And Barack and I were raised with so many of the same values, like you work hard for what you want in life. That your word is your bond; that you do what you say you're going to do. That you treat people with dignity and respect, even if you don't know them and even if you don't agree with them.

Michelle Obama

In his first term, President Barack Obama played a cautious manager navigating the worst economic disaster since the Great Depression and cleaning up the messes left by President George W. Bush in Iraq and Afghanistan.

Kevin O'Leary

My fellow Americans, you have to decide what kind of country you want to live in. If you want a you're on your own, winner take all society you should support the Republican ticket. If you want a country of shared opportunities and shared responsibilities - a 'we're all in it together' society, you should vote for Barack Obama and Joe Biden.

William J. Clinton

Barack Obama's inspirational whoosh to the presidency in 2008 was unusual. Most campaigns are less exhilarating; indeed, they are downright disappointing - until someone wins.

Joe Klein

And I love that even in the toughest moments, when we're all sweating it - when we're worried that the bill won't pass, and it seems like all is lost - Barack never lets himself get distracted by the chatter and the noise. Just like his grandmother, he just keeps getting up and moving forward... with patience and wisdom, and courage and grace.

Michelle Obama

I voted for Barack because he was black. 'Cuz that's why other folks vote for other people - because they look like them... That's American politics, pure and simple.

Samuel L. Jackson

Look at the coded language the Right is using against President Barack Obama. Openly calling him a liar in Congress, saying he is 'not a Christian, he was not born here, he is not one of us.' That makes addressing such issues trickier for the first African-American in the White House.

Jesse Jackson

When it comes to the health of our families, Barack refused to listen to all those folks who told him to leave health reform for another day, another president. He didn't care whether it was the easy thing to do politically - that's not how he was raised - he cared that it was the right thing to do.

Michelle Obama

That is who Barack Obama is - a person of admirable character - and that is who he has remained for me over these last four years. I have not agreed with his every decision, but never once have I seen him break his cool, lose his composure, or abandon his insightful perspective - even during the most serious and/or absurd national disasters.

Elizabeth Gilbert

Before Barack Obama took office, it looked like that pride could have vanished forever, but today, from the staggering depths of the Great Recession, the nation has had 29 straight months of job growth. Workers across my state and across the country are getting back the dignity of a good job and a good salary.

Ted Strickland

President Barack Obama has stood watch over the greatest job loss in modern American history. And that, my friends, is one inconvenient truth that will haunt this President throughout history.

Mitt Romney

What's missing is leadership in the White House. And the story that Barack Obama does tell, forever shifting blame to the last administration, is getting old. The man assumed office almost four years ago - isn't it about time he assumed responsibility?

Paul Ryan

Barack Obama would not be President if he were dark skin. You know what I mean? That's just the truth. I might not be as successful as I am now if I was dark skin.

J. Cole

I love that for Barack, there is no such thing as 'us' and 'them' - he doesn't care whether you're a Democrat, a Republican, or none of the above... he knows that we all love our country... and he's always ready to listen to good ideas... he's always looking for the very best in everyone he meets.

Michelle Obama

My parents shared not only an improbable love, they shared an abiding faith in the possibilities of this nation. They would give me an African name, Barack, or blessed, believing that in a tolerant America your name is no barrier to success.

Barack Obama

What if Barack Obama established a Presidential Advisory Committee that would meet once every couple of months, bringing together the former presidents for a conference in order to seek their collective wisdom? There is a wealth of experience in former presidents that generally goes untapped.

Tony Campolo

Every new president flatters himself that he, kinder and gentler, is beginning the world anew. Yet, when Barack Obama in his inaugural address reached out to Muslims by saying, 'To the Muslim world, we seek a new way forward, based on mutual interest and mutual respect,' his formulation was needlessly defensive and apologetic.

Charles Krauthammer

Electoral politics was always an objective of the Black Panther party, so Barack Obama is a part of what we dreamed and struggled and died for.

Bobby Seale

If you're looking for the safe choice, you shouldn't be supporting a black guy named Barack Obama to be the next leader of the free world.

Barack Obama

If you want a future of shared prosperity, where the middle class is growing and poverty is declining, where the American Dream is alive and well, and where the United States remains the leading force for peace and prosperity in a highly competitive world, you should vote for Barack Obama.

William J. Clinton

I think an overwhelming portion of the intensely demonstrated animosity toward President Barack Obama is based on the fact that he is a black man, that he's African American.

Jimmy Carter

I learned that the problems that we have are not solved by blaming somebody else, and that our hope is not in who governs us as a nation. It's not in Mitt Romney or Barack Obama or Ron Paul. Our hope is in the power of God and his gospel working in the hearts of people.

Kirk Cameron

The most enduring legacy of President Barack Obama is going to be a new generation of leaders standing up for liberty.

Ted Cruz

George W. Bush was a silver spoon dolt with no record to speak of other than bankruptcy and selling tropical plants, and we let him sail into the White House, but Barack talks about religious fundamentalism and guns being prevalent in poor areas, and we roast him for weeks?

Adam McKay

This nation has been through hard times. But those hard times have hardened our resolve. I'm ready to do the difficult work ahead. But I want to do that work with Barack Obama, and not a Tea Party ideologue. We can move America forward, but we can only do it together.

Harry Reid

So I'd be quite happy to have a three-hour Lincoln-Douglas-style debate with Barack Obama. I'd let him use a teleprompter. I'll just rely on knowledge. We'll do fine.

Newt Gingrich

In 2007, early in the improbable presidential candidacy of Barack Obama, the young first-term senator began a series of foreign-policy speeches that seemed too general to provide a guide to what he might do if elected.

Elliott Abrams

President Barack Obama's administration sometimes finds itself at odds with members of Congress who oppose nearly everything the United Nations does on principle.

Rebecca MacKinnon

Open government is, within limits, an ideal that we all share. U.S. President Barack Obama endorsed it when he took office in January 2009.

Peter Singer

Barack Obama has injected fresh momentum into efforts - stalled for a decade - to bring about nuclear disarmament.

Mohamed ElBaradei

When the American people elected Barack Obama and large Democrat majorities, the die was cast. ObamaCare was coming. Popular or not, constitutional or not, affordable or not, it didn't matter.

Bob Beauprez

I met Barack Obama, I read his book, I like him a great deal. I disagree with him on very fundamental issues.

Mark McKinnon

Barack Obama wants teacher service scholarships.

Nancy Gibbs

I think Barack Obama is one of the most exciting politicians to come along in a long time.

Mark McKinnon

I have no tax breaks or corporate interests to be supported by Barack Obama.

Adam McKay

Barack Obama is one of the greatest politicians in American history.

John Podhoretz

Barack Obama is the most famous living person in the history of the world.

Dee Dee Myers

There are many Israelis who are not keen on Barack Obama - they did not want to see him elected.

Richard Engel

If anybody ran a business like that they would be out of business quickly, and Barack Obama's leadership is driving this business, the United States of America, toward a fiscal cliff.

Chris Christie

President Obama is perhaps the most ideologically-motivated president in American history. But according to the ultimate authority, Barack Obama, he's a mere pragmatist.

Ben Shapiro

In Barack Obama, Democrats have put forth a man of strong religious faith who is comfortable connecting his spiritual life to his public role as a policymaker.

Mike McCurry

Let us now praise Barack Obama.

John Podhoretz

Should Sen. McCain capture the nomination as many assume, I believe this general election will offer the worst choices for President in my lifetime. I certainly can't vote for Hillary Clinton or Barack Obama based on their virulently anti-family policy positions.

James Dobson

Mr. Obama is proud of his belief that government knows best. When he told the world that individuals were not totally responsible for their personal success, that government has a major role in it, many Americans were taken aback. But Barack Obama sincerely believes that.

Bill O'Reilly

I like Barack Obama as a person. He's articulate, he knows sports, his brother-in-law's a coach. He always has the athletes to the White House. But I don't know about some of his policies and some of these people in Congress.

Pete Rose

Newt Gingrich would be a much better president than Barack Obama.

Rick Santorum

Just like Barack Obama, my views on gay marriage have evolved, and now I am a reluctant groom.

Edmund White

Barack Obama isn't the first politician to break a promise, torture the truth or outright lie to the American people. But, he certainly is among the most accomplished at it.

Bob Beauprez

Barack Obama hopes his famous health care victory will mark him as a transformative president. History, however, may judge it to have been his missed opportunity to be one.

George Will

President Barack Obama would do well to take a page or two from Clinton's playbook.

Dee Dee Myers

Barack Obama seems intent on enrolling more people on food stamps. Mitt Romney's focus is going to be on generating more jobs that will make food-stamps unnecessary for them.

Mike Huckabee

Perhaps we should wait until his second term begins before carving Barack Obama's face in Mount Rushmore. Is that asking too much?

Ron Fournier

Barack Obama is Occupy Wall Street. Barrack Obama is plugged into that world. That's what he believes.

Monica Crowley

Newt Gingrich would cream Barack Obama in a debate.

Monica Crowley

We need a direct repudiation of Barack Obama and everything for which he stands.

Monica Crowley

Facts matter. Science matters. Reason matters. Mitt Romney has shown an inability to respect any of the three. President Barack Obama not only respects them, he relies on them. He is an overwhelming and unquestioned choice to continue as president.

Eliot Spitzer

I think there's a lot of the hip-hop crowd behind Barack Obama because he's a black man. Honestly, I'm rooting for Hillary because race is only going to go so far. All the presidents are men at the end of the day.

Lupe Fiasco

The only thing growing faster than the federal government's deficit is Chris Matthews' man-crush on Barack Obama.

Tim Pawlenty

It has always seemed to me that Barack Obama has studied intensely and learned a great deal from Lincoln.

Tony Kushner

For eight years Republicans worked around the clock to delegitimize Bill Clinton. For the next eight years, Democrats tried to delegitimize Bush. Now Barack Obama is enduring the rage of his conservative opposition.

Joe Scarborough

But if I were to sum up who Barack Obama is and how he plans to meet this moment with one word, that word would be 'responsibility.' Responsibility to each other, our families, our communities, our country, and our world.

Valerie Jarrett

When you actually see Barack Obama, it's startling how slight he is and how young he looks.

Simon Hoggart

Stylistically speaking, Barack Obama could hardly be further from Jimmy Carter if he really had been born in Kenya.

Eric Alterman

Barack Obama is clearly a smart guy, talented.

Stephen Baldwin

If Barack Obama is elected, I'll be moving out of the country.

Stephen Baldwin

People want change. How is Barack going to do it? I think McCain can bring change.

Stephen Baldwin

Ever since John Kennedy, Democrats have had a weakness for dashing younger men like Bill Clinton and Barack Obama and, I suppose, Jimmy Carter. They balance their tickets with senior statesmen - Lyndon Johnson, Joe Biden, Walter Mondale. (Al Gore was young but played ancient).

Joe Klein

During his public life, Barack Obama has often referred to his biracial background and itinerant childhood and has said, 'In no other country on Earth is my story even possible.' True.

Monica Crowley

During the 2008 presidential campaign, Senate Majority Leader Harry Reid marveled at the electability of Barack Obama because, unlike previous black candidates, Mr. Obama was 'light-skinned' and lacked a 'Negro dialect.'

Monica Crowley

We can support President Barack Obama, because he supports us. We can support Barack Obama, because he shares our values and our vision.

Richard Trumka

Barack Obama knows that to create an economy built to last, we need to focus on middle-class families. Families who stay up on Sunday nights pacing the floor, like my dad did, while their children, tucked in bed, dream big dreams. Families who aren't sure what Monday morning will bring, but who believe our nation's best days are still ahead.

Chuck Schumer

Middle class people, I think they realize that Romney is not for them because of his narrowness, but they want to make sure that Barack Obama is focused on them with things that will make a difference. They know he tried, but they also know that it didn't do as well as they would have liked.

Chuck Schumer

To do health care was a noble, good thing, and it will help America dramatically. I don't begrudge Barack Obama choosing it, even though if I were president, I might not have.

Chuck Schumer

There are few tribes more loathsome than the American Right, and their vicious use of the shortcomings in the NHS to attack Barack Obama's attempts at health reform are a useful reminder.

Simon Hoggart

I believe Barack Obama has shown a deep conviction to help those most in need, even if their voices are not always the ones heard the loudest in Washington.

Ricky Martin

I like Barack Obama.

Bobby Seale

I've met a handful of presidents, from Jimmy Carter to Bill Clinton to George Bush to Barack Obama.

Jimmie Johnson

Ronald Reagan knew who he was. Barack Obama is still working through that equation politically.

Joe Scarborough

This is not a time for America to 'believe in magic.' This is a time to drive education forward. This is a time to drive the economy forward. This is a time to drive America forward. We must do it together. And we must re-elect Barack Obama as President of the United States.

Jim Hunt

Show me one single patriot who has ever been in Barack Obama's life in any position of influence. You can't do it... Barack Obama detests this nation as founded. He has zero respect for the founding documents.

Brad Thor

The question now is does Obama have any hope of raising money? I don't think he'll raise it out of the New York people, I don't think he's going to raise it out the Hollywood people, so where's the money going to come from for Barack Obama?

Juan Williams

During the campaign for re-election, Barack Obama at least made vague references to a willingness to accept $3 trillion of reduced spending in exchange for a $1 trillion dollar tax increase.

Bob Beauprez

The Romney-Ryan plan would replace the guarantee of Medicare with a voucher that wouldn't keep up with costs. Congressman Ryan says that he wants Medicare to be around for his grandkids. Well, if that's the case, he had better vote for Barack Obama!

Debbie Wasserman Schultz

Remember, the first presidential candidate to reject public financing for both the primary and general election was... Barack Obama, in 2008. He did it, in spite of a flat pledge to the contrary, because his campaign saw that it could vastly outspend John McCain.

Jeff Greenfield

I like that Barack got that job.

Hannibal Buress

One of the many, many salutary aspects of Barack Obama's impending presidential nomination is the sea change his victory marks in the battle for the mind-set of the American foreign policy establishment.

Eric Alterman

Given the pervasive secrecy of the Bush-Cheney administration, and the sorry consequences of that disposition, President Barack Obama's early emphasis on openness in government seems almost inevitable.

Noah Feldman

When people ask me why I'm amazed at what Barack Obama has accomplished, I tell them it's not because of what most of America and the world sees and knows of his history. It's because I witnessed what I can only describe as a bizarre turn of events that thrust him into position to even become a U.S. senator.

Don Lemon

The United States attorney in South Carolina was a Barack Obama appointee. Politically, he is to the left of Mao Zedong.

Trey Gowdy

I'm proud that Colorado delivered a victory to Barack Obama in 2008 and we will do so again in 2012.

Ken Salazar

The election of Senator Barack Obama brought jubilation across Africa, where millions celebrated him as 'one of their own.'

George Ayittey

Though there are many differences between Barack Obama and Jimmy Carter, they are strikingly similar in their poor economic records and even more so in their shared pessimism and bearishness on America.

David Limbaugh

Let's go tell everyone we meet that, when the American dream is at stake, you want Barack Obama in charge.

Deval Patrick

Well I think that, if you want to look at polarizing people right now, I wouldn't look at Palin, I'd look at Barack Obama.

Laura Ingraham

Events in America show the extent to which democracy there is fuelled by populism - Barack Obama's victory is a manifestation not of Washington's need for change, but of America's. That is not how democracy works in England.

Andrew O'Hagan

Barack Obama and Michelle Obama don't go to Georgetown... The Clintons did, indeed. And the Clintons go out and about in Washington now. They go to neighborhood restaurants.

Kitty Kelley

Just because everybody else is engaged in a group hug with Barack Obama doesn't mean that somebody doesn't have to tell the truth.

Joe Scarborough

Do you agree with me that we can't afford four more years of Barack Obama?

Rob Portman

Barack Obama and Jimmy Hoffa are like Tweedledum and Tweedledee, Lady Gaga and hype, the 'Jersey Shore' cast and hairspray: inseparable. The president can no more disown the Teamsters Union's leader than he can disown his own id.

Michelle Malkin

As he enters his final term, with the elegiac music playing out there in the distance, Barack Obama will use the history that he has come to embody and, perhaps, even to fulfill, as part of a larger project that never will be completed but only finished, over and over again.

Charlie Pierce

I've said it before: Barack Obama is really the president Richard Nixon always wanted to be. You know, he's been allowed to act unilaterally in a way that we've fought for decades.

Jonathan Turley

In theory, at least, all presidents are servants of the people who elected them. In the case of Barack Obama, it has seemed from the start that the idea as applied to him was more than mere metaphor. He is the first president in my lifetime whom the country felt obligated to remind that he know his place.

Charlie Pierce

Barack Obama has raised tons of money. That is what he means by being green.

Evan Sayet

President Barack Obama is a doer. And we in America will do big things with him.

Jim Hunt

Sam Nunn might bring us Georgia and maybe even another Southern state but, in my opinion, at an unacceptable cost to our principles and to the concept of change that has stirred millions to rise and work for Barack Obama. Sam Nunn would be a disaster as a running mate and a total anathema to millions of Americans.

David Mixner

I interviewed most of the presidential candidates about their positions on technology issues in the 2008 election. After those interviews I endorsed one candidate from each party - Barack Obama and John McCain. Neither of them were leading the primaries at the time, but they seemed like the best candidates, solely from a tech policy perspective.

Michael Arrington

When I first heard that Barack Obama was going to be the first black president, I wanted to do the smallest, biggest tribute in history.

Willard Wigan

A complete investment in the Obama administration required that any real opposition had to be demonized. The investment in Barack Obama had to be protected.

Bob Ehrlich

The hoary joke in the literary world, based on 'Dreams From My Father,' was that if things had worked out differently for Barack Obama, he could have made it as a writer.

James Fallows

We all know by now that Barack Obama is not a patriot. After all, he doesn't always wear a flag pin, and he objects to the idea that he should be required to in order to run for office.

Will Thomas

I'm a big fan of Barack Obama. I think he carries a heavier burden and is held to a greater and higher standard than other candidates : I think there's a large, large portion of this country that feels disenfranchised and marginalized by the political process.

Chris Carter

There are many people that frankly cannot get themselves to oppose Barack Obama. They make a lot of excuse for him.

Jonathan Turley

Congressman Berg will repeatedly talk about Harry Reid and Barack Obama, and I find it interesting, because this morning, when I woke up and brushed my teeth, I looked in the mirror and I did not see a tall, African-American, skinny man. So let's make it clear that my priorities are North Dakota priorities.

Heidi Heitkamp

Barack Obama has been the architect of policies that have hurt our country domestically as well as foreign.

Robert Pittenger

In the alternate universe of conservative talk radio, the killing of Bin Laden coincidentally happened on Barack Obama's watch. He had to be kicked dragging and screaming into authorizing it, and even then he made lots of mistakes.

Jackson Katz

Look what's happened to Barack Obama over the last two years or George Bush for eight. It's a blood sport. But at some point I may feel the need to run for office again.

Joe Scarborough

My concern about Barack Obama is he ran a campaign in 2008 where he said we're going to bring people together and solve big problems. And he specifically talked about the need to reach across the aisle and deal with issues like the economy, which was obviously the top issue in 2008. It has not happened.

Rob Portman

The biggest accomplishment, in racial terms, for Barack Obama was being elected. He had to overcome his blackness to be elected. He climbed the Mt. Everest of American politics, becoming an historic first.

Randall Kennedy

Two years before the last election you nor anyone else would have predicted that Barack Obama was going to get elected president of the United States.

David Axelrod

Today I am announcing my support for Senator Barack Obama for President of the United States of America.

Joe Andrew

Michelle Obama was asked when life begins. According to her it's when she and Barack take over the White House.

Evan Sayet

The more Americans find out about President Barack Obama's health care law, the less they like it. A majority of Americans want out.

John Barrasso

We can support Barack Obama because he's committed to putting America back to work with good jobs - and he proved it by saving the auto industry.

Richard Trumka

You could put all of Rev. Jeremiah Wright's angry sermons on to one loop. You could put that loop up on the big screen at Radio City Music Hall and let it play there 24 hours a day, seven days a week and Barack Obama will still emerge as the next president of the United States.

Gary David Goldberg

When Caroline Kennedy endorsed Barack Obama in 2008 as her father's rightful heir, she laid upon him the mantle of Camelot and the enduring mystique of John F. Kennedy, who, according to polls, continues to be America's most beloved president.

Kitty Kelley

Eisenhower was less deferential to the military than he seemed likely to be, Kennedy was not at all beholden to the pope, George W. Bush was smarter than portrayed and Barack Obama has not led a charge from the left - least of all on behalf of the civil liberties that have eroded since September 11, 2001.

David K. Shipler

I supported Barack Obama. I wasn't very quiet about my support. I thought he was going to be a refreshing change to George Bush. But what has happened is that we have an election that's become a single-issue election, and that issue is Barack Obama. And he's an icon to both sides.

Jonathan Turley

There's a misconception about Barack Obama as a former constitutional law professor. First of all, there are plenty of professors who are 'legal relativists.' They tend to view legal principles as relative to whatever they're trying to achieve.

Jonathan Turley

If Barack Obama goes on to win the election, there will be plenty of ink and video spent on chronicling the historic nature of the turnout among young voters and African-Americans. But as important as both constituencies have been to Obama - particularly in the primaries - it's Hispanics that could be putting him over the top on Nov. 4.

Chuck Todd

With the likely nominations of Barack Obama by the Democrats and John McCain by the Republicans, one of these two parties is headed for a 2009 crack-up that could prove as messy as any party civil war in recent history.

Chuck Todd

Barack Obama inherited a bankrupt economy, a bankrupt government, and a bankrupt foreign policy.

Thomas P.M. Barnett

With respect to Barack Obama, let's face it; Barack Obama is an iconic figure in the African-American community. We respect that. We understand that. African-Americans are going to vote for the first black president, especially when he happens to share the liberal politics on economic issues that many in that community hold.

Artur Davis

In Barack Obama, we have a great education president who is rebuilding America. His Race to the Top program is doing more to 'spur us' to improve our public schools than anything we've ever done as a nation.

Jim Hunt

Barack Obama is an economic patriot.

Ted Strickland

Barack Obama is betting on the American worker.

Ted Strickland

And one of the most important values of Barack Obama is that he will always level with the American people.

Charlie Gonzalez

People are not going to reelect Barack Obama. But will the new president govern as a real conservative? We're going to have to apply the heat to make sure.

Steve Forbes

I cannot imagine a worse job than being president of these Untied States in these most trying of times. President Barack Obama has been under siege from every side for the entirety of his time in office.

Beth Broderick

We need each and every one of you to commit to vote for Barack Obama today!

Jim Messina

We are ready to work hard, work together to re-elect President Barack Obama. We must do it because women deserve to make their own choices and determine the course of their lives.

Nancy Keenan

I ask Hoosiers to come together and vote for Barack Obama to be our next President.

Joe Andrew

In many ways I'm similar to Barack Obama, who also has a strange name but was raised by a white American mother. His background is far more complicated than his name would suggest. Furthermore, the fact that I was a child during the hostage crisis has caused me to equate being Iranian with being alienated.

Said Sayrafiezadeh

I have not heard from President Barack. I've never gotten a phone call.

Jay Pharoah

Interpreting anyone's marriage - a neighbor's, let alone the president's - is extremely difficult. And yet, examining the first couple's relationship - their negotiations of public and private life, of conflicts and compromises - offers hints about Barack Obama the president, not just Barack Obama the husband.

Jodi Kantor

This election isn't about Barack Obama or Mitt Romney. It's about you. The other guys write $10 million checks and make $10,000 bets. But we've bet this campaign on you.

Jim Messina

Barack Obama and I have an honest disagreement on the issue of abortion.

Bob Casey, Jr.

I know Barack Obama. And I believe that as president, he'll pursue the common good by seeking common ground rather than trying to divide us.

Bob Casey, Jr.

The very things that I would love about Barack and that you would love about Barack is that he is one of us. He's a normal guy. He's not a political animal.

Enrico Letta

When people see Barack Obama, they don't necessarily see an African-American president. They see someone who is a child of immigrants. They see someone whose family has worked hard and struggled. And they see many similarities between themselves and Barack Obama.

Grace Meng

There are some days when history is made. Yesterday was one - and I was honoured to be in Washington to watch Barack Obama being sworn in. During his soaring inaugural address, the new president gazed over a teeming National Mall that was crowded with more than a million people.

Des Browne

I don't know whether Barack Obama was born in the United States of America. I don't know that. But I do know this: that in his heart, he's not an American. He's just not an American.

Mike Coffman

I just worry a lot. I'm a worrier. Michelle and Barack are really dear to me. I mean, I love them. And I don't want to see them get hurt. Just the nature of politics is hurtful. So every time they are hurt, I get hurt. It's a lot to ask of people, and it's a lot to see your friends go through. It's hard not to get emotional.

Valerie Jarrett

Barack Obama won a second term but no mandate. Thanks in part to his own small-bore and brutish campaign, victory guarantees the president nothing more than the headache of building consensus in a gridlocked capital on behalf of a polarized public.

Ron Fournier

I represent the Democratic party... I've never been nor do I ever plan to be a John McCain supporter. I support Barack Obama.

Young Jeezy

Personally, I can't see the appeal in trekking down to D.C. for a networking extravaganza, even if it is built around a special moment in American history. While I find the election of Barack Obama inspirational, I don't have a desire to memorialize it with overly effusive celebration.

Jamie Johnson

Al Qaeda is still a threat. We cannot pretend somehow that because Barack Hussein Obama got elected as president, suddenly everything is going to be OK.

Barack Obama

For the first time in my adult lifetime, I am really proud of my country. And not just because Barack has done well, but because I think people are hungry for change. And I have been desperate to see our country moving in that direction.

Michelle Obama

Barack Obama is more irritating than the other nuisances on the Left.

P. J. O'Rourke

Barack Obama's administration responded to the Haitian crisis within 24 hours. Here comes the soldiers, here comes the food, go go go... Rush Limbaugh told his multi-millions of listeners that Obama only did that to gain favour with black people in America. This is the kind of idiocy that I have to deal with in my country.

Henry Rollins

If you felt that excitement when you voted for Barack Obama, shouldn't you feel that way now that he's President Obama? You know there's something wrong with the kind of job he's done as president when the best feeling you had was the day you voted for him.

Mitt Romney

I think Barack Obama is a socialist. I think he cares for his country - don't get me wrong about that - but I think he truly misunderstands what this country was based upon, the values that America was based upon, which was free enterprise and having the ability to risk your capital and having a chance to have a return on your investment.

Rick Perry

See, that's why Barack's running: to end the war in Iraq responsibly - to build an economy that lifts every family, to make sure health care is available for every American - and to make sure that every child in this nation has a world-class education all the way from preschool to college.

Michelle Obama

Barack Obama happens to be the first African-American, and so criticism of him is and always was gonna be racism, and therefore not permitted.

Rush Limbaugh

If you think the President was right to open the doors of American opportunity to young immigrants brought here as children who want to go to college or serve in the military, you should vote for Barack Obama.

William J. Clinton

The Democrats cannot find Romney fingerprints on what's happening to this country. Every fingerprint is Barack Obama's, Joe Biden's, Nancy Pelosi's, Harry Reid's, Barney Frank's, you name it, Eric Holder.

Rush Limbaugh

I am confident that when the facts and policies have been examined, when the record of performances have been reviewed, Barack Obama and Joe Biden will once again be elected to lead our beloved country to a better future.

Jimmy Carter

The President didn't offer any clarity in his latest speech about what he would do to tackle our nation's debt before it tackles us and it's still not clear how he'll keep Medicare from going bankrupt. One thing is clear though, Barack Obama isn't interested in governing or putting forward solutions to fix our nation's problems.

Paul Ryan

Think about one of the most powerful influences on a young child's life - the absence of a father figure. Look back on recent presidents, and you'll find an absent, or weak, or failed father in the lives of Lyndon Johnson, Richard Nixon, Ronald Reagan, Bill Clinton and Barack Obama.

Jeff Greenfield

When it comes to jobs, President Obama makes the Jimmy Carter years look like good old days. If we fired Jimmy Carter then, why would we rehire Barack Obama now?

Paul Ryan

On taking office in 2009, U.S. President Barack Obama put Israeli settlements at the center of U.S. policy in the Middle East.

Elliott Abrams

No one making less than $250,000 under Barack Obama's plan will see one single penny of their tax raised, whether it's their capital gains tax, their income tax, investment tax, any tax.

Joe Biden

Barack Obama's large contributor was Goldman Sachs - same thing on the Republican side. If you go to both their conventions, you see the same lobbyists paying off both sides so they win either way.

Jesse Ventura

Barack Obama makes me feel good to be a black man.

Snoop Dogg

My dear brother Barack Obama has a certain fear of free black men. As a young brother who grows up in a white context, brilliant African father, he's always had to fear being a white man with black skin. All he has known culturally is white. He has a certain rootlessness, a deracination.

Cornel West

A good day for Barack Obama is anytime the dominant topic of discussion is anything but the economy.

Bob Beauprez

After thousands of hours of news coverage, we have learned that Hillary is a liar and Barack is a terrorist or something.

Adam McKay

Wishful thinking won't make the Palestinians an Israeli peace partner, no matter how much President Barack Obama pressures Israel to make concessions; caustically mocking Putin's worldview won't make it any less real or mitigate the Russian threat.

Ben Shapiro

The person who takes the oath of office in the next four months will shape not just the next four years, but the next forty years of our nation. In these next four years, we need proven leadership, proven judgment and proven values. America needs four more years of President Barack Obama.

Rahm Emanuel

When the Soviet Union fell, optimistic scholars believed the world had shifted inexorably in the direction of free markets and liberal democracy. Instead, the West gradually embraced bigger government and weaker social bonds, creating a fragmented society in which the only thing we all belong to, as President Barack Obama puts it, is the state.

Ben Shapiro

You have to be an extremist to believe that you're gonna be the president of the United States and your name is Barack Hussein Obama! And he's using extreme methods, but his application is very smooth. Michelle Obama is extreme, her presence is extreme. And it's an extreme good. Extreme is not negative.

Mos Def

A disturbing prospect looms before us as Americans consider the possibility of a second term for President Barack Obama. Millions of conservatives who revere the Constitution, with its guarantees of freedom and limited government, have watched with alarm as the campaign season has unfolded.

James Dobson

I'm riding my man Obama. I think he's a visionary. Actually, Barack told me the first date he took Michelle to was 'Do the Right Thing.' I said, Thank God I made it. Otherwise you would have taken her to 'Soul Man.' Michelle would have been like 'What's wrong with this brother?'

Spike Lee

In 2008, I was one of the young feminist whippersnappers who voted for Barack Obama over Hillary Clinton in the Democratic primaries - or as many of my older counterparts called me at the time, a traitor.

Jessica Valenti

If you want to understand what is going on in the White House today, you have to begin with Barack Obama.

Dinesh D'Souza

Barack Obama has come closer than any figure in recent history to obeying a direct call of the people to the brutal and bloody fields of political mission.

Michael Eric Dyson

There is something uniquely depressing about the fact that the National Portrait Gallery's version of the Barack Obama 'Hope' poster previously belonged to a pair of lobbyists. Depressing because Mr. Obama's Washington was not supposed to be the lobbyists' Washington, the place we learned to despise during the last administration.

Thomas Frank

Are you ready to fight for good jobs and and a solid level playing field? Are you ready to prove to another generation of Americans that we can build a better country and a newer world? Joe Biden is ready. Barack Obama is ready. I am ready. You're ready.

Elizabeth Warren

With Barack Obama as president and the super-happening Michelle Obama as First Lady, you would think a new tone, a new tune, a kicky new jazzitude, would have entered Washington discourse, but it remains a landlocked island unto itself, held captive by its tribal fevers.

James Wolcott

Barack Obama is the most antibusiness president in a generation, perhaps in American history.

Dinesh D'Souza

If Barack Obama now, or some black person in the future, should become president, neither Jesse Jackson nor Al Sharpton would be out of a job. A black president can't end black misery; a black president can't be a civil rights leader or primarily a crusader for racial justice.

Michael Eric Dyson

Barack Obama is like the old joke about boats. The two best days of owning a boat are the day you buy it and the day you sell it.

Howie Carr

Let me tell you, Barack Obama is the most down dude in the world, but he's so smart; so articulate, such an amazing speaker; such a passionate man. He's humble.

Marlon Wayans

As an early-and-often chronicler of Chicago-on-the-Potomac, I am amazed at the stubborn and clingy persistence of President Barack Obama's snowblowers in the media. See no scandal, hear no scandal, speak no scandal.

Michelle Malkin

If he'd been negotiating Obamacare, Lincoln would have made the infamous 'Cornhusker Kickback' deal - $100 million in Medicaid funds for Nebraska to secure a Senator's vote - in a heartbeat, even if the press howled as it did when Barack Obama agreed to it, forcing its cancellation.

Joe Klein

But Barack Obama is not a person who would defend the rights and heritage of the European-American people.

David Duke

Only in America can a Barack Obama happen. Only in America can a Don King happen.

Don King

Barack Obama has talked a lot about changing the way America relates to the world, and few areas are as ripe for reform as our policies on foreign aid.

Iqbal Quadir

I'm asking you to talk with your friends, neighbors, and relatives - even the ones you've never talked to about reproductive rights. That's how you can throw your number in the bucket, and stand with a president who has stood with us. Conversation by conversation, vote by vote, we will re-elect President Barack Obama!

Nancy Keenan

Unfortunately, these past few years, you can work hard, try to be as successful as possible, follow the rules, and President Barack Obama will do everything he can to stand in your way.

Nikki Haley

Barack Obama was not born into wealth or privilege, yet today his is president of these United States of America. Barack Obama has lived the American Dream. He has walked in our shoes.

Ken Salazar

The Constitution I uphold and defend is the one I carry in my pocket all the time, the U.S. Constitution. I don't know what Constitution that other members of Congress uphold, but it's not this one. I think the only Constitution that Barack Obama upholds is the Soviet constitution, not this one.

Paul Broun

Yes, I have a website that puts out conservative news. Yes, I am part owner of a gun company. Yes, I'm a Republican who was cast into the limelight for having the temerity to confront Barack Obama on the question of redistributing wealth... But I'm a working man, and I'm working.

Joe Wurzelbacher

For four years, Barack Obama has been running from the nation's problems. He hasn't been working to earn reelection. He's been working to earn a spot on the PGA tour.

Mitch McConnell

Among the many international consequences of Barack Obama's stunning victory in the United States is worldwide introspection about whether such a breakthrough could happen elsewhere. Could a person of color win power in other white-majority countries?

Shashi Tharoor

Though the euphoria surrounding Barack Obama's election last week as President-elect has not yet begun to subside, it is already time to recognise that the most important challenge facing the next U.S. president is to restore America's standing in the eyes of the world.

Shashi Tharoor

I think that Barack Obama faces a level of divisiveness, and I don't mean on a national level in terms of the North and the South and the Civil War; I really mean just politically.

James Spader

The American people are desperately seeking a Moses to lead them out of the wilderness, back to the land of milk and honey. They thought maybe Barack Obama was the one, and when he proved to be mortal after all, they were willing to listen to anyone new.

John Yarmuth

My first 'SNL' episode was with Michael Phelps and Lil Wayne. And if you go back and watch the monologue - it was supposed to feature Barack Obama, but we couldn't get him - it was with William Shatner. But if you watch it, Guy Fieri is sitting in the front row.

Bobby Moynihan

We need to send Barack Obama back to Chicago. I'd like to send him back to Kenya, back to Indonesia. We have to unmask this man. This is a man that seeks to destroy all concept of God. And I will tell you what, this is classical Marxist philosophy.

Rafael Cruz

George W. Bush was a very bad president. The Iraq war was a big mistake. The U.S.A. needed a political change. I hoped Barack Obama could be a good president, but I'm disappointed. He hasn't done well.

Marc Rich

I could have possibly beaten Senator McCain in the primary. Then I could have been the candidate who lost to Barack Obama.

Mitt Romney

I think Barack Obama is a one-term President.

Dick Cheney

I knew Barack Obama, absolutely. And I knew him probably as well as thousands of other Chicagoans.

Bill Ayers

Barack is at a level where he can't - no matter how much he wants to or how much we want him to - he's not going to come take out our garbage, so to speak. He can't be the garbage man and the president. He can't be the mayor and the alderman. He can't fill all those roles. So I always push for local, local activity on the political scene.

Lupe Fiasco

Christ would not vote for Barack Obama, because Barack Obama has voted to behave in a way that it is inconceivable for Christ to have behaved.

Alan Keyes

'You're stupid,' is not something even his most severe critics usually say to President Barack Obama.

P. J. O'Rourke

The realities are that, you know, as a black man, you know, Barack can get shot going to the gas station, you know.

Michelle Obama

You know, out-of-touch liberals like Barack Obama say they want a strong economy, but in everything they do, they show they don't like business very much. But the economy, of course, is simply the product of all the businesses of the nation added together. So it's a bit like saying you like an omelet, but you don't like eggs.

Mitt Romney

I love that we can trust Barack to do what he says he's going to do, even when it's hard - especially when it's hard.

Michelle Obama

None of what Barack Obama is doing or wants to do to this country is anything the rest of the world hasn't seen before and already failed at.

Rush Limbaugh

Is it a coincidence that in 1998, Barack Obama talks about a majority coalition of welfare recipients and in 2012 we got a record number of Americans on food stamps while he's president? I don't think it's a coincidence.

Rush Limbaugh

The greatest hope most Americans - including Republicans - had when Barack Obama was elected president was that the election of a black person as the country's president would reduce, if not come close to eliminating, the racial tensions that have plagued America for generations.

Dennis Prager

If you want to know what the biggest thing in your way to an improved standard of living, higher pay, a more rewarding career is: Barack Obama and the Democrat Party and their economic policies. They are the roadblock.

Rush Limbaugh

Even non-democratic allies no longer trust America. Barack Obama has alienated our most important and longest standing Arab allies, Egypt and Saudi Arabia. Both the anti-Muslim Brotherhood and the anti-Iran Arab states have lost respect for him.

Dennis Prager

For the last five years, we have been presented with the idea that Barack Obama is superhuman. Barack Obama is unlike any of us or anyone else. And he isn't. In fact, he's much less achieved and much less accomplished than most who have gotten half as far as he has, and I think maybe what we saw was the best.

Rush Limbaugh

For me, Barack Obama's election was a milestone of the most extraordinary kind. On the day he was elected I felt such hope in my heart. I thought we were seeing the beginning of a new era of equal opportunity across race and gender such as America had never known before.

Jesse Jackson

Supporting the definition of marriage as one man and one woman is not anti-gay: it is pro-traditional marriage. And if support for traditional marriage is bigotry, then Barack Obama was a bigot until just before the 2012 election.

Marco Rubio

I will focus on being substantive and I will focus on Barack Obama.

Newt Gingrich

After Barack Obama won the 2008 presidential election, I was heartened to see him issue an Open Government Initiative on his first full day in office.

Jesse Ventura

Barack Obama did tell me that I was one of Michelle Obama's favorite actors.

Dwayne Johnson

Barack Obama is probably the most exciting candidate that either the Democratic or Republican party has produced at least since I've been around. He's fresh, he's new, he's insightful.

Joe Biden

The only two men I have time for are Barack Obama and my trainer.

Sophia Bush

So my one kid's 4, my other kid's 4 months, I'm 44, Barack Obama is the 44th president - it's all lining up nicely here.

Eddie Vedder

Folks know that while I respect Barack Obama and do not cheap-shot the president, I am very skeptical of his big government, nanny-state philosophy.

Bill O'Reilly

A troubled economy is always the sitting president's fault. It was when Ronald Reagan defeated Jimmy Carter, when Bill Clinton defeated George H.W. Bush, and when Barack Obama defeated John McCain by running against George W. Bush.

Mark McKinnon

Never mind what you've heard. Halle Berry was not the first black woman to win an Academy Award for Best Actress. She was actually the 74th white one. And never mind all this talk about America electing its first black President; Barack Obama is actually the 44th white man to hold the job.

Jeffrey Kluger

Obama killed Osama. Yes, President Barack Obama gets to crow about the killing of Osama bin Laden.

Mark McKinnon

Income inequality has gotten worse under President Barack Obama.

Timothy Noah

I think that it's important that the American people know that Barack Obama didn't have a mild association with Bill Ayers, he had a very strong association with Bill Ayers. Bill Ayers is not someone that the average American wants to see their president have an association with.

Michele Bachmann

I want Barack Obama for president. I love Obama. I call Palin the helicopter huntress from hell! I want my children to have a wonderful future, and it's disturbing when I look around. Americans aren't very well-liked. A likable president would be a great start.

Pamela Anderson

I don't pay a lot of attention, frankly, to what Barack Obama says.

Dick Cheney

Electing Barack Obama president was a glorious Jackie Robinson moment for the United States of America. Obama didn't just win; he became the first Democrat since Jimmy Carter to win a popular-vote majority.

Timothy Noah

Barack Obama is many things; among them, he is a tough and even ferocious political warrior.

Jon Meacham

In 2008, Barack Obama did get Democrats hyperventilating, whipped up to a creamy froth, while John McCain creaked ahead like a cranky granddad whom Republicans let move to the front of the buffet line, deferring to seniority, as they had in 1996, when Bob Dole turtled to the top of the ticket.

James Wolcott

The grass roots are energized because the absolutely highest priority in the country in November is to defeat Barack Obama. I have spoken with literally thousands and thousands of tea-party activists - I have yet to meet a single tea-party leader that is not going to vote for Mitt Romney.

Ted Cruz

The Tea Party emerged from a laudably grassroots base: libertarians, fervent Constitutionalists, and ordinary people alarmed at the suppression of liberties, whether by George W. Bush or Barack Obama.

Naomi Wolf

You know, let me be very clear. I supported Barack Obama originally.

Bernie Sanders

I was never a fan of Barack Obama's bipartisanship routine.

Thomas Frank

Barack Obama has brought glamour back to American politics - not the faux glamour-by-association of campaigning with movie stars or sailing with the Kennedys, but the real thing. The candidate himself is glamorous. Audiences project onto him the personal qualities and political positions they want in a president.

Virginia Postrel

On the Left, the best and brightest go into politics - Barack Obama is the epitome of the perfect leftist. On the Right, the best and brightest go make money. Very few conservatives want to endure all the nonsense you have to put up with to run for office.

Ted Cruz

The tactics of Saul Alinsky and Barack Obama are geared toward wealth redistribution.

Monica Crowley

That distinctive presidential conduct is now gone forever, banished to the snows of yesteryear by Barack Obama. From the beginning of his presidency to the present, he has spoken specifically and in unprecedented fashion of Republicans as his rivals, his stumbling blocks, the primary cause of his troubles.

John Podhoretz

If his presidency is to represent the full power of the idea that black Americans are just like everyone else - fully human and fully capable of intellect, courage and patriotism - then Barack

Obama has to be subject to the same rough and tumble of political criticism experienced by his predecessors.

Juan Williams

Barack Obama's decision to come out in favour of gay marriage may be a historic occasion, but it is not an isolated one. His administration has been making pro-gay noises for some time; his demographic in the upcoming election is young and educated, precisely the group that favours equality for the LGBT community.

Edmund White

I admired the way McCain worked on campaign finance reform. I admired the way Nancy Pelosi stiffened the Democrats' spine during the health care debate. I admire the way Barack Obama has raised a dog in the White House without ever putting it on the roof of the car for a vacation drive.

Gail Collins

I stand before you tonight as a young American, a proud American, of a generation born as the Cold War receded, shaped by the tragedy of 9/11, connected by the digital revolution and determined to re-elect the man who will make the 21st century another American century - President Barack Obama.

Julian Castro

Barack Obama may have found the answer to his biggest rhetorical challenge: When millions of voters are unemployed or underemployed, how does a president simultaneously sound realistic and optimistic?

Ron Fournier

We're Americans. We shape our own future. Let's start by standing up for President Barack Obama.

Deval Patrick

Dig just a little bit deeper. Work just a little bit harder. And don't get weary! Remember this is personal! Let's finish what we started, and re-elect President Barack Obama!

Debbie Wasserman Schultz

The birthers, the fanatics, the people running around in right-wing militia and Aryan support groups, it is unbearable to them that President Barack Obama should exist.

Sheldon Whitehouse

There were lots of smart black people at Harvard before Barack Obama, but none of them ever got to head up the law review. There has been a history of discrimination.

Andrew Young

Barack Obama is not Harry Truman, who dropped the A-bomb on Japan to stop World War II. Barack Obama is not John F. Kennedy, who lowered marginal tax rates to get economic growth and job creation. Barack Obama and the far left, they are a completely different ball of wax.

Monica Crowley

It has been my honor to support and work with President Barack Obama, a man who has brought courage and character to the presidency. President Obama's strength of character leads him to do the right thing, even when it isn't the easy thing.

Harry Reid

I don't really feel McCain. It ain't just because Barack is black; he can make change. Just like Bush equals recession, Barack equals progression.

Young Jeezy

Barack Obama's life was so much simpler in 2009. Back then, he had refined the cold act of blaming others for the bad economy into an art form. Deficits? Blame Bush's tax cuts. Spending? Blame the wars in Iraq and Afghanistan. No business investment? Blame Wall Street.

John Sununu

You could argue that Barack Obama faced in '08 a situation as bad as any president since the Great Depression. What Obama inherited from the Bush administration, we all remember, was just an absolute global catastrophe.

Tony Kushner

If half-black Barack Obama had decided years ago to call himself white - which his genes certainly entitled him to do - his story would have carried very different meaning. If millions of part-black people had followed him into whiteness, then the N.A.A.C.P. would be in true crisis.

Eric Liu

Something very significant appears to be happening in America. There is a dramatic shift in voter affinity toward the GOP, and it may prove to be the mountain-too-high for Barack Obama's campaign.

Bob Beauprez

I am convinced that I do not want to give up more power to the White House, whether it's George Bush or Barack Obama. And I'm going to fight as hard as I can against President Obama on these earmarks and my Republican colleagues who hate to vote for them, but love to get them.

Harry Reid

I was starstruck by Michelle Obama. She's an amazing-looking lady, and I'm a massive Barack Obama fan anyway.

Niall Horan

I'm here tonight, not as a Republican, not as a Democrat, but as an optimistic American who understands that we must come together behind the one man who can lead the way forward in these challenging times: my president, our president, Barack Obama!

Charlie Crist

This November, with the re-election of President Barack Obama, this generation of Americans will ever expand upon the hope, the truth and the promise of America.

Cory Booker

Barack Obama likes to point to General Motors as the poster child for the job creation success of his economic policies. However, whatever your sentiments about the government's bailout of General Motors, for every job Barack Obama 'saved-or-created' in the U.S. there were two jobs off shore.

Bob Beauprez

There's something about Barack Obama that induces Americans to imagine what they cannot see. The Right envisions a vile socialist, while many on the Left picture an inspired liberal, politically restrained in his first term but now free to pursue his true beliefs.

David K. Shipler

If you have spent any time with Barack Obama, you know he's a funny guy. He's a good guy. He knows sports.

Ed Rendell

If you take a guy like a Barack Obama, who's raised millions of dollars from the most donors in the history of this nation, it suggests that there's a deep and profound hunger for a new politics to come forth. And a guy like him has been able to mobilize that and to reach certain parts of the hip-hop generation.

Michael Eric Dyson

Mitt Romney says he believes in America and that he will restore American exceptionalism. I have news for him, we already have an exceptional American as president and we believe in Barack Obama.

John F. Kerry

One thing without any question that is true today and that is that the winner of the 28-minute commercial is President Barack Obama.

Tim Scott

According to the people who dearly would love to throw him out of office, Barack Obama was elected to be 'above politics.' He wasn't elected to be president, after all. He was elected as an avatar of American tolerance. His attempts to get himself reelected imply a certain, well, ingratitude.

Charlie Pierce

Since the global economic crisis began, the change in global attitudes is clear to see - and I think it is pitiful. Barack Obama came to China and he is probably the only president of the United States never to mention the words 'human rights' in public.

Ai Weiwei

America is about to turn the page on Barack Obama's four-year experiment in big government.

Mitch McConnell

In the depth of the near depression, that he faced when he came in, Barack Obama and Democratic leaders in Congress provided 'recovery funds' that literally kept our classrooms open. Two years ago, these funds saved nearly 20,000 teacher and education jobs - just here in North Carolina.

Jim Hunt

Barack Obama is the worst President in history.

Ben Quayle

Previous presidents, including great ones like Roosevelt, have used the IRS against their enemies. But I don't think Barack Obama ever wanted to be on the same page as Richard Nixon.

Joe Klein

I don't know anyone at the highest levels who approved Abu Ghraib. If President Barack Obama for a moment thought that somebody at a high level had approved it, he would go after them.

Peter T. King

Folks, do you agree with me that we cannot afford four more years of Barack Obama?

Rob Portman

Barack Obama's class warfare will not work on this Republican nominee. Not in Utah.

Mia Love

We can move America forward with a strong middle class. We can move America forward with a strong Democratic majority in the Senate. And together we can move America forward with Barack Obama in the White House.

Harry Reid

The clearest way to cut some of this fiscal drag would be to extend the current payroll tax holiday and increase it - as proposed by President Barack Obama. This would cut the fiscal drag by almost half.

Mark Zandi

I would also say Barack Obama has spent much, much, much, much more money than the Republicans.

Jonah Goldberg

Tell me why the limousine fleet has increased by 42 percent since Barack Obama took office. Why are we spending taxpayers' money on that? Limos should be for weddings and proms, certainly not for government officials to be riding around in.

Mark Neumann

Take a stand against intolerance and for our American values. Say it with pride: I support democracy in America. I support working people in America. I support opportunity in America. And I support Barack Obama for another four years as president of the United States of America!

Richard Trumka

I think Barack Obama has brought a new level of ethical standards to Washington. Has he changed some basic hard-knuckle politics? No. You need hard-knuckle politics to succeed.

Ed Rendell

At the end of the day, the only things that are shovel ready around here are the words coming out of Barack Obama and Joe Biden's mouth.

Reince Priebus

Barack Obama is an elegant and literate man with a cosmopolitan sense of the world. He is widely read in philosophy, literature, and history - as befits a former law professor - and he has shown time and again a surprising interest in contemporary fiction.

Teju Cole

Don't worry, America. We survived Jimmy Carter, and we will survive Barack Obama. Only one questions remains... who is the next Ronald Reagan?

Kathleen Troia McFarland

Under President Barack Obama, the Congressional Hispanic Caucus has been invited into the White House and given a seat at the table. Hispanics are serving in unprecedented numbers at the highest levels of this administration, including in the Cabinet.

Charlie Gonzalez

I see my job simply as helping disseminate the message of Barack Obama, working with the communications team to make sure that we're true to the ideals and the values and the programs that he wants to advance in this country. And that's the extent of my involvement.

David Axelrod

As our values are the core to who we are as human beings, they are also the easiest way to identify and connect with others in meaningful ways. Think about it - most political campaigns are based around values. Barack Obama's 2008 election campaign galvanized millions of youth behind two very clear values - hope and change.

Adam Braun

It's been so long since a talented writer last occupied the White House; no wonder, then, that American writers have been among the most prominent of all the demographic groups claiming a piece of Barack Obama for themselves.

Jonathan Raban

I think Barack Obama and his team believe that the federal government is best prepared to handle virtually everything in our lives. I mean, they're socialists in every respect of the word and I think they'd like to take over everything in our lives if they could, including health care.

Mark Neumann

We pursued the wrong policies. George Bush is not on the ballot. Bill Clinton is not on the ballot. Mitt Romney is on the ballot, and Barack Obama is on the ballot. And Mitt Romney is proposing tax reform, regulatory reform, a wise budget strategy and trade. The president has proposed tax increases.

Glenn Hubbard

A lot of people who voted for Barack Obama expected and were led to expect something new in politics: a new tone of political discourse in Washington. And I think - I think they're disappointed, because Barack Obama is not a new kind of politician. In fact, he's an old Chicago politician.

Bernard Goldberg

Being in Harlem on the night of Barack Obama's election was extraordinary. It was the best street party I have ever gone to, and it felt like the period of American history which began with slavery had ended that evening.

Hari Kunzru

Mitt Romney saying that Barack Obama gets an F is one of the most ridiculous things that he has said in this race.

Stephanie Cutter

When Barack Obama is right, then I'll support him. When he is wrong, I'll fight him.

Paul Broun

Barack Obama and Joe Biden have been working hard to help middle-class families make it in America.

Steny Hoyer

Barack Obama's official nomination as the Democratic Party's standard-bearer was a very poignant moment for millions of Americans. As the first non-white major party nominee, Obama is carrying a big load on his shoulders. He's holding the hopes and dreams of a lot of folks who thought the presidency was only reserved for white men.

Chuck Todd

People don't think about the fact that when Barack Obama's parents had him - it was illegal for them to be married in several states in this country. So if we start making it okay that certain people can marry and other people can't, it's a slippery slope of civil rights. Who knows who is going to be allowed to marry or not marry next.

Kerry Washington

During the 2008 campaign, I strongly endorsed Barack Obama for president. I did so early, when many Democratic leaders - including many prominent African-American politicians - believed the safe bet was to back then-front-runner Hillary Clinton.

Douglas Wilder

Quite frankly, Barack Obama knows what it's like to pay a mortgage and student loans. He knows what it's like to watch a beloved family member in a medical crisis and worry that treatment is out of reach. Barack Obama knows our struggles. And, my friends, he shares our values.

Ted Strickland

As much as the Democrats try to change the subject, this election will be about Barack Obama, period. Mitt's speech last night hit all the right notes, but this fight is not about him. He's just the vessel. Now the question is, does this guy at 1600 Pennsylvania Ave. who thinks the private sector is doing fine get another four years?

Howie Carr

I'm a registered independent. I don't really believe in political parties. Bottom line: Mitt Romney's tax policy helps me. But I can't stomach seeing somebody go hungry or somebody not being able to get an education because I want more. So, I'm supporting Barack Obama.

Brian J. White

I was with - he wasn't the president then, but - Barack Obama, when he was running, in Washington, during Black Congressional Caucus Weekend, and did a panel about global warming with him. It was almost as if I switched careers for a while, and became a political activist.

Lawrence Bender

Barack Obama is a threat to the continued existence of the United States, and he must be impeached, or resign.

Kesha Rogers

Barack Obama says that we need to be humble toward terrorism. Yet he is the one we have been waiting for. That is humble?

Evan Sayet

Ten percent of the American population thinks that Barack Obama is a Muslim. Those are the people that have not learned the skill of filtering information from the vast barrage of inaccurate information that we're all faced with everyday. I think that's a very 21st century skill.

Michael Azerrad

President Barack Obama has it right - there is a lot to change about Washington. The problem is, not much will get changed unless we confront the runaway filibuster in the U.S. Senate.

Peter Fenn

I would say that Barack Obama has always been a real optimist about what can be accomplished. He believes that government can be used to create systemic, long-term, real change. And the first lady is more of a skeptic.

Jodi Kantor

The enemy is not me. The enemy is Barack Obama.

Robert Pittenger

I don't think that a vote for Barack Obama is a symbolic thing. I think it's much more than that. It's not just a black man. It's not just a feel-good vote. It's the idea of electing someone who really does want to make a difference.

Aunjanue Ellis

Barack Obama is crazy sexy.

Mircea Monroe

Was Sen. Barack Obama a Muslim? Did he ever practice Islam? The presidential candidate officially rejects the claims, but the issue of Obama's personal faith has re-emerged amid conflicting accounts of his enrollment as a Muslim during elementary school in Indonesia, the world's most populous Muslim nation.

Aaron Klein

Well, the chairman of Federal Reserve just made his move to rescue Barack Obama. We're gonna have QE3. We're gonna print some more money.

Rush Limbaugh

So what is so strange about saying I want Barack Obama to fail if his mission is to reconstruct and reform this nation so that capitalism and individual liberty are not its foundation? I want the country to survive. I want the country to succeed.

Rush Limbaugh

Few expected very much of Franklin Roosevelt on Inauguration Day in 1933. Like Barack Obama seventy-six years later, he was succeeding a failed Republican president, and Americans had voted for change. What that change might be Roosevelt never clearly said, probably because he himself didn't know.

Russell Baker

The only people who live in a post-black world are four people who live in a little white house on Pennsylvania Avenue. The idea that America is post-racial or post-black because a man I admire, Barack Obama, is president of the United States, is a joke. And I hope no one will even wonder about this crazy fiction again.

Henry Louis Gates

In 2008, Barack Obama had all the wind at his back, everything going for him. He was an African-American at a time when the country was eager to do that. The Republicans had, in the view of many of us, pretty much disgraced themselves at home and abroad for eight years.

George Will

I actually never thought that Barack Obama was anything but a typical Democratic party politician, which to me meant that he was probably in bed with Wall Street.

Matt Taibbi

One of the things about leadership is that you've got to show up. And if you want to be president of the United States you've got to make a case to the American people that Barack Obama needs to be dismissed from his position.

Tim Pawlenty

Category after category, Barack Obama hasn't met the promises that he laid out to the American people.

Reince Priebus

Unless and until Barack Obama addresses the full depth of Americans' anger with his full arsenal of policy smarts and political gifts, his presidency and, worse, our economy will be paralyzed.

Frank Rich

Barack Obama is not a man of The Gut, and it is driving official Washington crazy. This is a good thing, because resisting The Gut is what the Constitution is all about, especially in its war powers, which this president is conspicuously contemplative about exercising, at least in every context except launching drones.

Charlie Pierce

From education to broadband, from building roads and bridges to supporting the military, Barack Obama is delivering for North Carolina. And he is delivering for America. A growing middle class is the foundation for a strong America.

Bev Perdue

Barack wants to stop all children from working on the farm... Can you imagine this? I just, I can't fathom that. Did you ever think we'd grow up in America and see something like that? Let me take it one step further. He wants to disallow the 4-H from training children to work on a farm.

John Raese

Hillary Clinton and Barack Obama are two peas in the same pod, and the American people have tasted that, and said, 'Look, that's not a good taste.'

Mitt Romney

There's no question in my mind that I think I would have been a better president than Barack Obama has been.

Mitt Romney

Barack Obama doesn't think this country should be number one. If it were number 35 it'd be fine with him.

Rush Limbaugh

Barack Obama, foreign policy wizard. I just have to laugh.

Rush Limbaugh

Barack Obama's enemies are the people who make this country work. Barack Obama's enemies are those who succeed. Those are the people whose income he wants to redistribute. Those are the people whose income he wants to take, using the power and the force of the federal government to do it.

Rush Limbaugh

It is Barack Obama who is at war with this country. Recent events prove it. This is not a cliche. It's not a figure of speech. Obama is at war with the U.S. economy.

Rush Limbaugh

Virtually nothing Barack Obama has done has left America or the world better since he became president. Nearly everything he has touched has been made worse.

Dennis Prager

Under Barack Obama, the only 'Change' is that 'Hope' has been hard to find. Now millions of Americans are insecure about their future. But instead of inspiring us by reminding us of what makes us special, he divides us against each other. He tells Americans they're worse off because others are better off. That people got rich by making others poor.

Marco Rubio

Barack Obama doesn't believe in free enterprise. He's never going to admit it. For instance, he's never going to come straight out and say, 'If you own a business you didn't build it.' Alright, maybe he will.

Marco Rubio

Barack Obama is way smarter than Bush - so way, way smarter than me. Obama is way more charismatic than me.

Penn Jillette

President Obama is the kind of politician who puts promises on the record, and then calls that the record. But we are four years into this presidency.The issue is not the economy as Barack Obama inherited it, not the economy as he envisions it, but this economy as we are living it.

Paul Ryan

Barack Obama's military triumphs will come neither in long wars nor even short ones, but in a series of raids.

Elliott Abrams

Pinochet and Barack Obama both have the same primary goal, and that's to be president and stay president as long as allowed.

Viggo Mortensen

www.ingramcontent.com/pod-product-compliance
Lightning Source LLC
Chambersburg PA
CBHW071230280526
45787CB00002B/871